MINDS MAP

The Journey To Ignite Life's Inner Spark

KAIZEN
LIFE SPARK

Charlotte Mills

MindShift Map

THE JOURNEY TO IGNITE LIFE'S INNER SPARK

Charlotte Mills

ISBN: 1974297918
ISBN-13: 9781974297917

Contents

Introduction

—∞∞∞—

First and foremost, I would like to commend you for making this investment in yourself, for stepping into your inner world and rewarding yourself with knowledge. To know that you care about yourself and value your time to prioritize yourself in this demanding world is empowering.

In *MindShift Map*, I will guide you through a map of information and strategies, taking you on a path of self-discovery to spark a mind shift in your life. By learning and implementing these strategies, we will ignite the spark of continuous improvement to your existence.

As we start on this journey, it's important we get to know each other. I am a Kaizen Life Spark coach.

What on earth is Kaizen Life Spark?

Kaizen is the Japanese philosophy of continuous improvement.
Life is our existence.
Spark is to ignite, activate, or kindle spirit.

I am a coach who believes that a combination of the above is what we need to explore more of in our lives, including in our relationships, careers, health, mission for financial freedom, and overall well-being. It is essential that we strive for positive change, and sometimes it's not easy. Sometimes we need to be ignited or *re-ignited* in some of these areas.

I have been coaching since 2005 in wellness and fitness, but I have shifted my focus to Kaizen Life Spark since 2014. Leading others to gain clarity on vision, personal efficiency, and existence is one of the most rewarding contributions I have ever made. I work with people to help them ignite their spark so they can create the flame of their chosen existence and carry the torch into their desired reality. This, in my model of the world, is where we find our sweet spot.

Throughout *MindShift Map*, we will be able to find out what you would choose to continuously improve given the opportunity, and we will raise the question of presence and self-awareness in your life. So please, take the opportunity to resonate with the words and find meaning in the reflection of your own path.

Why Kaizen Life Spark?

—⊸∞⊷—

FOR ME, THIS IS WHERE it all began. Everything I ever learned led me to create the Kaizen Life Spark Method. It changed my life.

It is super important to me because I understand the power it has to stimulate change for the better, and it provokes growth like I've never seen or experienced before.

Kaizen Life Spark set me on a path to self-discovery, and for that, I will always be grateful. I found a new perspective on this game of life and have never looked back. This newfound knowledge took me to another level. The crazy part is that it feels like it should have all been common sense (but as we know, common sense is not always too common). That's the greatness of *MindShift Map*. It provides you with building blocks to better understand yourself and the world that surrounds you.

Before Kaizen Life Spark, I was always reading and traveling with determination to find "something." I never really believed in the cliché of "searching to finding oneself." I was looking for something to keep me engaged and inspired. Perhaps it was my purpose I was looking for. I was continually falling into the same patterns. I would travel to different countries frequently, but when I did stay in my home country, I worked for different companies. Even within the same company, I would change roles or locations on a regular basis. I rarely stayed in one place for more than six months to one year maximum.

Now, please don't misunderstand me; I loved it. I thrived on the change, a new challenge, the opportunity, and the excitement of something new—a new country, a new environment, a new team, a new day. As much as I loved it, there was still "something" missing. I wasn't fully satisfied, no matter what I was doing.

Over time, I started to become very aware of my lack of ability to settle. I have never been a fan of that word—*settle*: to remain in one place, to stay a certain way. To me, it just seemed dull and uninspiring. I always believed, and still do, that there is more out in the world to see and to achieve. However, I was ignorant in how to channel this belief to get the balance I had been craving.

By using the strategies outlined in *MindShift Map*, I was able to reflect on the true reality of my life. I was able to realize that through all the change and instability I had, there was consistency in my need and passion to help others. Aside from moving around so much, I was still in the same industry and managed to keep long-term relationships with people I met over the years. I had the ability to stay committed regardless of the chaos, and now I have learned how to have the satisfaction, balance, and inspiration I was looking for. The "something" I was looking for was already inside of me.

This sparked a new reality for me where I could see and feel my own potential, a potential that woke me up like a bolt of lightning on a cold and stormy night. This wake-up call has held me accountable ever since, because *now* I know better. Now that I know better, I cannot make excuses or go backward. It is really as simple as "If I know better, I can do better."

Kaizen Life Spark *MindShift Map* only works if you are ready for this phase of your life. As I mentioned before, once you know better, there is no going back. I invite you to welcome a new spark into your life. I have witnessed people in real depths of darkness as well as those already content with their lives move to new realms as a result of these learnings. *MindShift Map* will give you the tools to build the foundation to create the life you desire.

Congratulations for already respecting and loving yourself enough to read this and being open to the possibility there is more to learn than what you already know. Here's what a previous client had to say after working through *MindShift Map*:

After completing *MindShift Map*, I can honestly say my eyes have been opened and my world has expanded. I have been completely unaware of how my actions have been destroying my progress not just in my work life but my personal life too. I was always so angry and thought my way of doing things was the only way. I was not open to listen to others unless they held a certain status in my opinion. Working through this book has helped me see that I was so closed off. If I open up to new ways of doing things, then maybe I wouldn't be so angry all the time. I now know what I must do, and I now know I am the only one who can do it. No more excuses, no more playing the blame game—from here on out, it's all about me.

Kaizen Life Spark *MindShift Map* will empower you to make your desires a reality—if you're ready.

How to Navigate
MindShift Map

———— ✺ ————

To get the most out of *MindShift Map*, please read each section thoroughly in sequence.

There will be "Reality Checkpoints" throughout the Map. They are strategically placed at the end of each section for maximum impact. These Reality Checkpoints are thought-provoking take-aways. Take your time at each Reality Checkpoint to complete the exercise. There are no wrong answers, but there is always an answer within you.

To have the full Kaizen Life Spark MindShift experience, please ensure you move on to the next section only when the Reality Checkpoints are completed. At the back of this book, there are some blank "Playbook Journal Pages." Use these pages as a journal to complete your Reality Checkpoints.

Take as much time as you need to complete the checkpoints. They are not designed to be rushed; they are designed to be reflected on in as much depth as possible. Sometimes it can be overwhelming to spend so much time looking into our inner world and going into new depths. This is completely normal, and the solutions will be there by the end of the journey.

The journal will become your playbook for life by the end of *MindShift Map*. It will be the most empowering book you have ever created.

Reality Check

———∞∞∞———

*The first step to a sparked life is understanding the
here and now, deciding kaizen is the way forward.*

—KAIZEN LIFE SPARK

THE HERE AND NOW IS essentially all we've got in the present moment.
Do we really understand what that means for us? When was the
last time you took time out of your day and reflected on what your
reality looks like? Now, I don't mean sitting with a cup of coffee
for ten minutes and thinking in general. When was the last time
you zoomed out and looked at the big picture of your life, broke
it into segments, and really assessed where you were at?

In this section, we are going to see if you are ready to welcome new learnings into your life. We will understand and recognize what it means to be conscious; we will begin to understand
why some people fail and why you will not fall into that trap. We
will discover what empowerment really is and how it influences
our personal responsibility. Finally, in this section we will engage

in the wheel of spark, which will guide insight into your current reality in all aspects of your life.

To be able to develop ourselves, we must have a foundation to build upon. We can only have a true starting point if we are aware of our current position. Research has shown that increasing self-awareness can reduce your number of blind spots by 20 percent, thus boosting your personal growth. Reality checks give us the baseline we need and a benchmark for the future.

My world used to be full of ideals relating to progress and improvement. But when I learned the reality-check strategies, I realized my ideals of progression and improvement were not built from a solid foundation. This meant they didn't have the strength they needed to thrive. For example, I always felt like there was more to do and areas to improve, but I had no real understanding of what I really meant. I had no direction on what I wanted to improve or where I wanted to go. There was no direction in what way to progress, which meant I was either wandering aimlessly or carelessly following others. A reality check was exactly what I needed.

Some of my clients have worked through the reality-check section and realized they were not teachable, even though they always thought they were open to learning. After working through the Reality Checkpoints, they noticed some patterns in their own behaviors. They realized they must change in order to grow; otherwise, they would be stuck in the same position for the rest of their lives, and that was a scary thought.

You will discover this as a dawn of a new beginning. It is an opportunity to understand your current reality and baseline for growth. This will be a true reflection of *your* here and now. Be kind to yourself, embrace it, and learn from it.

Are You Ready to Learn?

———✺———

If you are not teachable, you are not coachable,
and that means we cannot help you.

—Robert Simic

So much knowledge is out there in the world, yet I still meet people who believe they know everything. There is nothing more limiting in this life than to think we know everything on any given subject. I strongly believe everyone I meet knows something I don't. It is literally not possible to know everything there is to know. Every day is a school day. Learning is how we become richer and wiser. We are about to find out if you are coachable—meaning, open to learning and ready for change.

Throughout the MindShift Map, I'd like to invite you to welcome each subject with an open mind for new learnings and new insights. Here is your first Reality Checkpoint.

REALITY CHECKPOINT

Some of the questions below may sound similar, but please read them carefully, as they have different meanings.

Answer the following questions on a scale of 0–10 (0 Low–10 High).

You are welcome to make notes, but please ensure you answer using the number scale. Keep a record of your notes and results in the Playbook Journal Pages at the back of the book.

For Example:

What are you willing to do?

* An example of 10/10: "I am willing to do anything to learn. I will ask questions, talk to strangers. I will pay. I will do anything to learn."
* An example of 2/10: "I am not willing to spend extra time. I am not willing to do more than the minimum required."

1) What is your willingness to learn?
2) What are you willing to do?
3) How much time are you really willing to invest?
4) How much time are you willing to put in?
5) How much money are you willing to spend?
6) What are you willing to give up?
7) What is your willingness to change?
8) How ready are you to change?

MindShift Map

9) How accepting are you of change?
10) What is your willingness to change how you think?
11) What is your willingness to change how you feel?

Well done for completing your first Reality Checkpoints! By answering these questions, you now have a true indication of how ready you are for the next steps in your MindShift Map journey.

If your answers were less than 10/10 in any given area, please be aware you may not learn as much as you could. If your journey is as important as you suggest, your score would be 10/10 every time. If it's not, please consider the points you scored lower and understand why. For example, if you scored a 5/10 on any of the questions, ask yourself, "Why didn't I score myself a 10/10? What can I do to be all in on this journey?" Take some time now to think about how you could become more committed to learning and change. Why are you reading this? What is driving you to seek further growth in your life?

Throughout this MindShift Map journey, the score may change as you become invested in the subjects at hand. These questions are relevant in all areas of life, not only the MindShift Map. The more open you are, the more you will gain.

If you did not complete the Reality Checkpoints, I urge you to ask yourself and understand why by using the questions above.

This is crucial for maximum results as you move throughout the MindShift Map journey, and this was *your* investment. I encourage you to go back and complete the Reality Checkpoints now before we move on to the next section. This will give you

7

the full Kaizen Life Spark MindShift Map experience. You will also have your playbook for life at the end, which you can reflect on and use as a base for the future.

Waking Up

—∞∞∞—

*Are you sleepwalking through life, or
are you coasting on autopilot?*

—Kaizen Life Spark

Is being on autopilot such a bad thing? Have you ever noticed yourself going through the motions, not thinking too much, and daily life continues as we know it? I have heard many people talk about this with such negative connotations. My question is, do we really understand what is happening to us when autopilot strikes? Here it is.

Have you ever arrived at your destination and realized you hadn't really thought much on how you got there? For example, driven a car to work but been so invested in your own thoughts or the music on the radio that you haven't noticed yourself changing gears, signaling, accelerating, or braking? Or have you ever stopped to think about every breath you take? Or which muscles you have to contract to digest your food?

Well, this is autopilot. This is our brain and body working in tandem unconsciously to complete a task. Our minds are so competent at executing these tasks that we are not required to consciously think of every detail. This is an incredible example of brain power and only a taste of our human potential and what we are capable of. Experts live in this stage of being. It can be amazing. (This is what we call stage 4 of waking up.) But if we spend too long in this stage of "unconscious competence" without learning anything new, this is where the negative connotations kick in and we start sleepwalking through life.

Be bold and begin to understand the different stages available to you.

Stage 1
Before reading this, I'm sure many of you had never heard the term *Kaizen Life Spark*. Before encountering this phrase, you didn't know it existed or what it meant. Therefore, you didn't know what you didn't know. This is otherwise known as "blissful ignorance." This is the stage where we learn something new. We are "unconsciously incompetent" or completely unaware of what we don't know, like a newborn baby.

Stage 2
We then move into the stage of discovery. Now you have heard of Kaizen Life Spark, but do you know the depth of what it means? Most people stay in this stage for most of their lives. We call this "conscious incompetence." Have you ever been in a conversation and somebody starts talking about something you know nothing

about? Some people will simply nod along without learning anything (stage 2), but others will ask questions to learn (stage 3).

STAGE 3
The more questions we ask and the more we learn about a subject, the deeper our level of understanding and sense of knowing will be. This is where we have the opportunity to become "consciously competent." The more we choose to ask questions and develop ourselves in a given subject, the faster we will move into the expert mastery stage of "autopilot" (stage 4).

STAGE 4
Autopilot describes this stage perfectly. Think about something you do automatically without a second thought. Take breathing as an example. When we breathe, we do not think about every detail. Our brain and body work perfectly together to ensure we can breathe easily. We are competent at this, and we are doing it unconsciously. If you have habits that you do unconsciously that do not serve you, it is time to consider if you want to be in autopilot. If not, break the habit by working through the stages to create habits you want.

The waking-up stages are relevant in all areas of our lives and can differ somewhat. For example, I can be on autopilot (sleepwalking—stage 4) when I'm at home, and I can be at work not learning or growing because I'm nodding along in meetings and not asking questions (stage 2). This is only one example, but for maximum results, we should identify which stage we are in for all areas of our lives, including career, relationships, romance, friendships, personal growth, rest, health, fitness, relaxation, and so on.

REALITY CHECKPOINT

1) Choose an area of your life you feel needs improvement.
2) Review it and decide which stage you find yourself in.
3) What can you do to move into the next stage?

For Example:

1. I feel like I need to improve my communication skills when I'm at work if I want to progress.
2. I find myself going through the motions every day. I know there are lots of courses I could do to take me to the next level, but I haven't enrolled in any. This is stage 2. I know I'm not competent in communicating but feel like I've been stuck.
3. I can push into stage 3 and gain knowledge on how to communicate more effectively. Then I will continue to practice what I've learned. By enrolling and completing the course, I will become consciously competent.

Failure

———⚬⚬⚬———

*Failure is only the opportunity to begin
again, only this time more wisely.*

—HENRY FORD

FAILURE HAPPENS FOR MANY REASONS. Here are my top five observations of why people fail.

1. Soft Foundation
   To build anything, we need a solid foundation; we need to create an environment conducive to success. We must ensure we are ready for what is to come. Accepting it will take all we have got, and our minds must be able to support any potential outcome. Creating a platform for growth is key.

   You are already one step ahead, as you are building your foundation by working through this MindShift Map. You are discovering your baseline, will know where to begin, and create the strong foundation for you to move into the world you desire.

2. Inner World

   Most people fail because they do not invest enough in themselves. Investing in their inner world must be priority to keep emotional and intellectual congruence with the intention at hand. We must invest time and knowledge to stay on top of our game. Inner work is the greatest work we can ever do. It will enable you to create new habits and ways of thinking and to learn new skill sets that will keep the spark ignited.

   We all know someone who has purchased a book or course and never started it. This is a common behavior of people who do not invest fully. Their intention is present, but the essential action is absent. Besides money, investment includes time and commitment. You have already begun to nurture and advance your inner world simply by using the MindShift Map.

3. Self-Sabotage

   Allowing the mind to wander into traps of influence is the fast route to failure. Listening to others who do not support the mission or indulging in one's own self-doubt and procrastination will compromise any form of success. If time is spent building a foundation and working on the inner world, then self-sabotage can be avoided with ease. Other tips to avoid self-sabotage include the following:

   ◆ Surround yourself with like-minded individuals who share and support your desires.
   ◆ Master your mind.
   ◆ Become an expert in your field.
   ◆ Be confident in your ability to figure things out.
   ◆ Manage your time effectively.

4. Unwillingness to Change
   Dreaming the dream and not being willing to do what's necessary is a shortcut to failure. When embarking on success, we must let go of any fears that could hold us back. Many people experience a fear of loss, either of what they currently have or what they could lose in the future, which leads to becoming stuck. Imagine if we thought about what we could gain instead. Being self-aware at this stage is crucial.

   I have witnessed countless numbers of people with potential to progress in their work but fear what their friends would think when they get the promotion, so they play down their skills and become comfortable where they are even though they are yearning to move forward. Fear will hold us back if we allow it to. What if they got the promotion and their friends were proud and inspired by them?

   The Waking-Up Reality Checkpoints help to identify areas in your life that need more attention.

5. Insufficient Energy Expenditure
   Exerting energy to places of low value is a common factor in failure. Move away from what you "don't want" and shift and focus energies to what you "do want." The more energy spent in the inner world will reflect in the outer world.

   For example, one of my clients really wanted to be in a relationship, but she kept failing. When we looked closer, it was because she was so afraid of what she didn't want and had lost sight of what she wanted. She was focusing on "being closed off" so she could not get hurt instead of "opening up to the possibility of meeting someone to love." Once she flipped this energy and thought channel, she found the man of her dreams within two weeks!

The Wheel of Spark and Keeping the Spark Alive sections of *MindShift Map* will help you strategize in these areas.

The reality is, everybody fails at some stage in life. What matters is what happens thereafter.

REALITY CHECKPOINT

1. What would you choose to do if you knew you would not fail?
2. What needs to be in place for you to achieve this?
3. What do you need to learn to achieve this?

Blame Game

———— ❦ ————

Blame is a scapegoat for the unenlightened.

—Kaizen Life Spark

There comes a time when we have to take personal responsibility for our results to become truly empowered.

We all know friends or colleagues who always have bad things happening "to" them. It is never their fault. There is always someone else to blame.

Have you ever spilled a cup of coffee and blamed the person who made it for filling up the cup too much? Have you ever blamed the traffic or missing your train for being late? Have you ever blamed your job for making you tired or unfulfilled? Have you ever felt unhappy about a situation and blamed someone else?

Take a moment to think: "I am the cause of my results." What questions does this lead to? "How could I have done better? Am I happy with this result? What could I do differently next time?"

Immediately, this gives us the power to make a difference in our own lives.

Perhaps if I wasn't in such a hurry and paying more attention to what I was doing, I wouldn't have spilled my coffee. If I had left the house earlier or checked the travel schedule before I left, then maybe I wouldn't have been late. If I quit my job and actually worked on something I loved, maybe I would be more fulfilled. If I went to the gym before work, maybe I would feel more energized.

If we continue to blame others for our results, we give away all our personal power to the person we are blaming. We leave the result up to him or her. Why would anyone want to leave his or her fate up to someone else? Once you recognize your own outlook—and I implore you to do so—you can challenge your own results.

It's our life and our responsibility to lead it.

If we don't like the result, let's go back to the drawing board and do better. This is far more effective than playing the victim by blaming others.

If we are not the cause of our own results, how can we ever be helped?

REALITY CHECKPOINT

1) Can you think of any situation in your life at the moment where you are blaming someone or something else for the outcome?

2) What could you do to help change the outcome?

3)   What could you do differently in the future to get a different result?

Wheel of Spark

—∞∞—

If you don't have time for the small things,
you won't have time for the big things.

—Richard Branson

Life can be a complex matter with lots of different areas intertwined. Using the Wheel of Spark will allow you to put those areas into perspective for yourself. By using this strategy, we will be able to identify what is important to you and how much balance you currently have in your life. We will look at your satisfaction levels so you can understand how happy you really are. As you work through the different areas of your life, please consider *your* top eight only.

Reality Checkpoint
Before you start, read the instructions and check out the example wheel below.

1. Label the eight segments on the Wheel of Spark with the top eight areas in your life.

(Some examples could be love, hobbies, social health, environment, spiritual development, and intimacy.)

2) Review your overall satisfaction in each area. Use a scale of 0–10.

Zero is at the center of the wheel and means Not Satisfied at All.

Ten is on the rim of the wheel and means Highly Satisfied.

3) Draw a dot to represent your score.

4) Join up the dots.

Example: The Wheel of Spark below shows not only some areas of satisfaction but some areas that need attention as well.

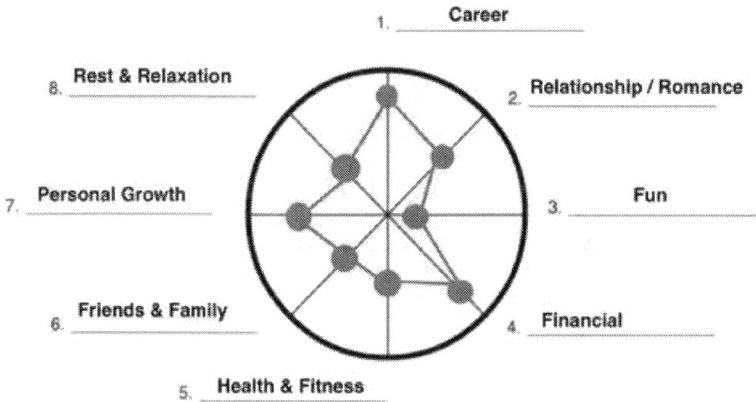

1. Career
8. Rest & Relaxation
2. Relationship / Romance
7. Personal Growth
3. Fun
6. Friends & Family
4. Financial
5. Health & Fitness

Take your time to complete *your* Wheel of Spark. This exercise should be completed with true, honest reflection. Complete your wheel below.

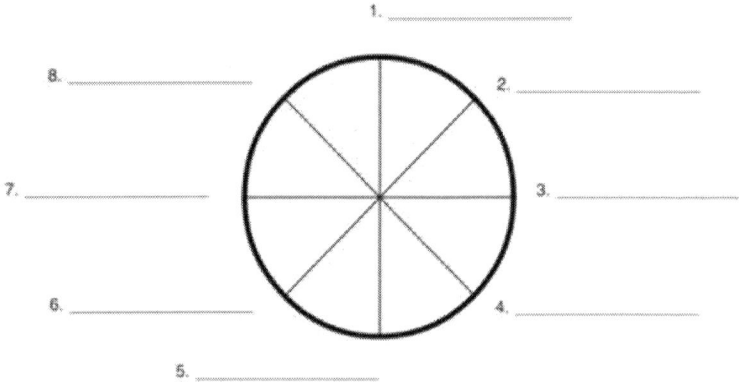

If you have completed the Reality Checkpoint above, you should now have an image showing all aspects of your life that are important to you. You should see a line within the wheel.

Does your life look in balance?

Are there areas showing low satisfaction?

Are there areas that need more attention?

Don't worry; we will come back to our Wheel of Spark as we move through our journey with the strategies to transform it to what we desire. For now, it is important that we see our here and now.

SECTION 2

Building a Foundation

———— ∞∞∞ ————

*Your future is built on a bedrock of your
inner world. To build anything of value,
we must create strength at the core.*

—KAIZEN LIFE SPARK

THIS SECTION OF THE MINDSHIFT Map will plant the seeds of the inner world and give you tools to add strength to your foundation. We will give you the basis in which reality is founded; how the mind processes information; and how we choose to listen, think, and feel.

Nothing incredible is born without the conditions being suitable. A flower will not grow unless the environment is fertile, seeds are planted, and it is watered. This underpinning knowledge will help you understand how to create a platform for growth in your world.

I misunderstood my world before having this knowledge. I didn't understand how the mind worked; I'd never really thought about it before. I was living naively. I believed that everyone saw things the way I did, and anyone who didn't was the "weird one," not me. Don't get me wrong: I respected other people's beliefs and opinions, but I always thought the majority of people saw the world the same way I did. I was going through life not really thinking about how I saw the reality in front of me. I wasn't thinking about how I thought about events or why I like the things I like. I just took for granted that the thoughts were there and this was "me," the life I'd been given. Little did I understand about the brain and how we process information or the almighty power our brains actually have to be able to decide everything for ourselves. It's mind-blowing to think some people never master their own minds and discover the potential they already have inside.

These learnings led me to many light-bulb moments that challenged the way I now see my world. It gave me the basis to forge my own reality, to one that serves me and those I love. You will notice I refer to "my model of the world" throughout the rest of the map because it is simply that: the way I see the world and what these lessons have taught me. This MindShift Map opened my eyes, and I am eternally grateful for the reality I see today.

Others who have followed the MindShift Map have been shocked to understand the way they have been looking and behaving in their lives. Some have realized they gave away all their power and control to their "five-year-old unconscious mind" too many times. They have discovered new ways of thinking and understanding themselves and are now in control of their world.

This section will help you to discover your baseline, where to begin in creating a strong foundation for you to move into the world you desire. You will see *your* model of the world.

Reality versus Reality

———⚬⚬⚬———

*Reality is merely an illusion, albeit
a very persistent one.*

—ALBERT EINSTEIN

DO YOU EVER WONDER WHY you can experience the same moment with someone but have a completely different result of the experience? For example, you watch a movie with your friend. She comes out feeling motivated and inspired, yet you come out wondering what it was all about, completely unaffected.

This happens because our minds process data differently. The data we sense (hear, see, touch, smell, and taste) is the same as what everyone else experiences. Very quickly, the data enters our minds, and then it becomes our own interpretation of the data. We add meaning to it based on what we believe to be true. What we believe to be true is all based on what we call our conditioning. Conditioning is the sum of our past experiences, learnings, memories, models of the world around us, attitudes, and internal beliefs.

Once we attach meaning to the data, we react to it. We create an emotion or a state based on the data we have interpreted, which in turn gives us our behavior and result to our "reality."

For example, if you touch a stove and burn yourself, you're less likely to touch a stove again. It is the brain's way of protecting us from what can hurt us. This is a very basic example of human nature and how some responses become automatic. However, if another person touched the stove when it was switched off, he or she would not have the same expectation, as he or she would not get burned, and therefore he or she is more likely to do it again. This results in two different people having two different beliefs about the stove.

There have been many studies on twins who were separated at birth and went on to live contrasting lives. These studies have shown that even when two people with identical genetics are put into different environments, their lives can become complete opposites. The people around them, the schools they attended, and their physical surroundings are contributors to who they are today and the lives they have created as a result of their conditioning, despite their genetics.

This is the same in our daily life, with the small encounters and the bigger encounters that we face. Just because we think something, it does not always mean that everyone will agree. This is because we have been conditioned differently through our own life experiences. What we learn to see on the outside becomes a reflection of what we really see and believe on the inside.

We have the amazing gift to identify these results and behaviors, which gives us the power to change our reality to one that serves us and those we love. Creating our own reality gives us ultimate responsibility for the way we think, feel, and respond in daily life. The human mind has the freedom to transform at any given moment we choose.

REALITY CHECKPOINT

1. What reality in your life do you wish was different?
2. What would you need to believe inside for this to change your current perceived reality?

Would You Listen to a Five-Year-Old?

───⊗⊗⊗───

*We all have voices in our minds that talk to us on
an almost constant basis. We must raise our level
of consciousness to better serve ourselves.*

—KAIZEN LIFE SPARK

DO YOU HEAR VOICES IN your mind? If you say no, then I'm not sure I
believe you. It's very common! I am talking about self-talk. Do you
talk to yourself?

Most people have experienced the analogy of the devil on
one shoulder and an angel on the other. One voice in their mind
is encouraging the right choices, and the other is encouraging the
wrong choices in any given situation. Who wins in this scenario?

Many would agree that most of the time, we choose the voice
that gives us the fastest solution and instant gratification; however, it is not necessarily what we require in the long term. Can

you relate? Perhaps the moment you talk yourself out of going to the gym? Or the moment you choose your favorite chocolate over a piece of fresh fruit?

In my model of the world, there is no devil or angel. There is simply me...and a five-year-old. Yes, that's right—a five-year-old! Allow to me to explain.

As soon as I became aware of this, my self-talk became more interesting and way more productive. Every time I had a situation and felt a voice encouraging the "wrong" choices for me, I looked at it as a five-year-old. Now don't get me wrong, there are many smart five-year-olds out there, and we all need advice from kids sometimes. But I questioned, if I had a five-year-old in front of me, would I be taking advice on my life choices? Highly unlikely—so why would I listen to this voice in my mind?

I then learned another interesting theory. I learned that approximately 95 percent of our minds work unconsciously (unaware) while only 5 percent work consciously (aware). I realized *I* was the 5 percent conscious voice, and the 95 percent unconscious mind was the five-year-old! Incredible—95 percent of the time, my mind and my life was being run by a five-year-old on autopilot!

We all have this set up in our minds whether you are aware of it or not. Now, you may not relate to my example of a five-year-old taking your 95 percent autopilot seat; however, it is important that you find a way to relate to the 95 percent of yourself that is your default setting. This is what our minds fall back to when we are not 100 percent focused toward what we want.

Your five-year-old mind—or your 95-percent-unconscious mind—has the following responsibilities and executes the list below automatically all the time. As you read through the list, ask yourself if you would want a five-year-old to be responsible for these tasks:

- Storing and organizing your memories
- Controlling your emotions
- Repressing memories with unresolved negative emotions
- Keeping repressed emotions for protection
- Running your body
- Preserving your body
- Following and enjoying orders
- Controlling and maintaining your perceptions
- Generating, storing, distributing, and transmitting energy
- Maintaining instincts and creating habits
- Taking everything personally
- Not processing negatives directly
- Working on the principle of least effort—will always do as little as possible

This theory really helped me understand that being conscious and simply paying attention was not only necessary but it was also going to determine my future! Remember what we learned in the first section, waking up to our stages of consciousness? Ninety-five percent of our mind is working in stage 4. It is crucial, and it is our personal responsibility to create the life we want, not merely to inherit the life we've been given and allow our unconscious mind to run without conscious input.

REALITY CHECKPOINT

1. What is your mind doing 95 percent of the time? What is your autopilot doing?
2. What do you need to be more aware of to ensure this 95 percent is serving you?
3. What will you do to become aware of behaviors driven by your unconscious mind?

For Example:

1. When I'm on autopilot, I am going for the easy options, I avoid anything I fear, and I keep myself to myself.
2. I need to acknowledge when I'm doing this and call myself on it every time it happens. I need to question if I really want to avoid the situation. If I face the situation, maybe I could grow and actually have what I want.
3. I will write a note every time I notice it happens throughout the day. I will look back on my notes each day or each week and see if I am becoming more conscious of my behaviors and set actions to improve.

Perception Is Projection

—⚬⚬⚬—

*A negative thinker sees a difficulty in
every opportunity. A positive thinker sees
an opportunity in every difficulty.*

—ZIG ZIGLAR

OUR UNCONSCIOUS MIND IS VERY resourceful and executes a lot of tasks at once. One of the responsibilities it holds is controlling and maintaining perceptions.

The *Oxford English Dictionary* defines perception as "the ability to see, hear, or become aware of something through the senses." As we have learned from the reality-versus-reality theory, we actually interpret the data our sense gives us. The mind tells us stories.

When we buy into our thoughts and listen to the story our mind is telling us, this is what happens in our brain:

Reality—what we think is actually happening
The Truth—we believe it
Important—we think it should be taken seriously and paid attention to
Orders—should be automatically obeyed
Wise—we know best
Threats—we should be frightened by them

However, it is important to recognize that our thoughts may be merely *sounds, words, stories,* bits of *language, true* or *not true, important* or *not important, wise* or *not, not* automatically followed.

Thoughts are *never* the following:

Orders—to be obeyed
Threats—to be frightened by

It is crucial to accept that this is *just a story.* Your mind's job is to tell you stories and anticipate trouble.

Therefore, when we interpret the perceptions, we are choosing what we want to see. What we see on the outside reflects what's on the inside. We see what we want to see. We will always look to prove ourselves right. If you look for a problem, you will find one. If you look for a solution, you will find one.

REALITY CHECKPOINT
Write what these quotes mean to you:

1. "Your perception of me is a reflection of you; my reaction to you is an awareness of me." —Anonymous
2. "Everything that irritates us about others can lead us to understanding ourselves." —Carl Jung

Thoughts

—∞∞∞—

Change your thoughts and you change your world.

—Norman Vincent Peale

In my model of the world, thoughts are one of the most powerful forms of energy there is. Thoughts are the birthplace of ideas—good ideas and bad ideas. Anything you can think of once started off as a thought in someone's mind. Think of the Wright brothers. They started with a thought of air travel and went on to invent the airplane. Mark Zuckerberg and three of his classmates had a thought to connect people online and went on to create Facebook. These are game-changing thought leaders.

Some thoughts will change the world, and yours can, too, if you want them to. We have thousands of thoughts every day. Some of them serve us and add value to our lives, and some don't. When we believe in our thoughts, we feed the thoughts with emotion and meaning, some positive and some negative. We then act on the thoughts. We either dismiss them because we don't believe in them, or we continue the thought pattern. As soon as we apply behavior, thoughts and ideas come to life and take form.

The action from our thoughts comes from what we believe to be true. The Wright brothers believed in their thought and that their idea could change the world. Therefore, they behaved congruently with their belief. They researched, they worked, they tested, and they bought their thought to life.

The same goes for thoughts that do not serve us. Thoughts have the power to change the world, but they also have the power to paralyze us. Many people who have committed suicide have done so because their thoughts took over. Some of them chose to buy into those thoughts and believed so strongly that there was no other option or thought available to them and that suicide was the only answer. This all stems from a thought. Mental illness is a serious issue, and anyone suffering should seek professional support. Being aware of thoughts can be a step toward relief for anyone who is struggling.

If we choose to buy into our thoughts and believe them, we behave in such a way that will turn the thought into existence.

Why am I writing all this?

Because thoughts are just thoughts. We have the power and capacity to recognize them as just that. We choose to act on them as we see fit.

However, I know people who still find themselves a slave to their own thoughts. They are not consciously choosing which thoughts will run their results.

The following are questions to ask yourself to understand which thoughts are serving you or not:

* Have I had this thought before?
* Do I gain anything from listening to this thought again?
* Do I benefit in any way from this thought?
* Does this thought help me take effective action?
* Does this thought help me be the person I want to be?
* Does this thought help me build the relationships I'd like?
* Does this thought help me connect with what I truly value?
* Does this thought help me create a long-term, rich, full, and meaningful life?

The following are techniques to help try when unhelpful (five-year-old self-talk) thoughts start:

* Thank your mind—"Thank you for that thought, but I won't be paying attention to that today."
* Don't take it seriously—For example, replace a serious word with a funny word. Instead of "I'm an idiot," replace with "I'm a banana." Immediately, it has no power.
* Sing your thought—Add a musical jingle to remove the intensity of the thought. For example, sing it in the "Happy Birthday" or "Jingle Bells" tune.

Give some of these tips a try. It is time to step up and not be afraid to see thoughts for what they really are.

REALITY CHECKPOINT

1. What thoughts do you have that you wish you did not?
2. What new meaning can you give to the thought?
3. How will you respond next time you have a thought that does not serve you?

Story of Your Life

—∞∞—

Most people do not listen with the intent to understand; they listen with the intent to reply.

—STEPHEN R. COVEY

THIS SECTION IS ABOUT YOU! Sometimes it's hard to find someone to really listen to us, so today that person is going to be you. Listen to yourself. Until you begin to consider your own life story, it will be tough to ignite a new spark. Even if you're not looking for anything new, these reality checkpoints will help you to discover or refresh your current life story.

My model of the world shifted when I began to look into my inner world using the Reality Checkpoints you are about to experience in this section. As I mentioned earlier in this book, I struggled to find that "something" that was missing. This section helped me to identify, categorize, and understand my baseline needs, which were the baby steps into discovering what that was.

I gained insight into what needed to change in my life. I understood what I really needed and what I was telling myself to be true. I learned to consciously be able to choose the meanings I gave to my memories, attitudes, and beliefs. This was special. Nothing could hold me back. I gained true clarity about what action needed to be taken and became increasingly resourceful in what I had to offer the world.

The strategies we use are not about telling the story of the past. It is solely about the life story of your future and opening your eyes to the possibility of what it could be. You will look into your inner world to understand what you have learned from your memories, what your desired attitudes are, and what you believe to be true about yourself. This will help you gain insight into your new playbook for life.

One of our MindShift Map graduates had this realization after completing the Reality Checkpoints in this section:

My main focus in life was my career. I kept destroying my relationships because I refused to work less, as my career was everything. Out of my six basic human needs, four were being met through my career, which left little time to focus on my relationships. After learning that my needs determined my focus, I was able to find a balance. I found other things to fulfill my needs, and now my world feels like it's in harmony.

There has never been a more crucial time to do the Reality Checkpoints in this MindShift Map.

What Do You Need?

———◦◦◦◦———

*Once we master our human needs, we
gain a wave of direction and an incredible
driving force to push us forward.*

—KAIZEN LIFE SPARK

IF I ASKED YOU TO answer "What do you need?" with no framing, I wonder what that list may look like. We all think we need to have or do certain things, but why do we think we need these things? We think we need them because we've learned over time from our past experiences. If you really do "need" them, only you know. We create such a sense of urgency when we say we need something. But what strategy was ever used to decide this, other than our conditioning? When did you last sit down and really think about what you need and why?

I'm writing about this theory inspired by the great Tony Robbins and Abraham Maslow's hierarchy of human needs. When I learned and applied this theory from my coach, another great,

Robert Simic, it was a game changer. So I want to share the basics with you.

There are six basic human needs that our bodies require to function efficiently and survive. This is true for every human being. The needs are as follows:

* CERTAINTY: the need for safety, stability, security, comfort, order, predictability, and consistency
* VARIETY: the need for surprise, challenges, excitement, difference, adventure, or change
* LOVE and CONNECTION: the need for communication, attachment, connection, intimacy, or love
* SIGNIFICANCE: the need to have meaning; to feel special, needed, and wanted; or to have a sense of importance
* GROWTH: the need for constant emotional, intellectual, or spiritual development
* CONTRIBUTION: the need to give beyond ourselves and care for, protect, or serve others

Our neurology requires these needs to be met. The level of each need's importance will vary from person to person, but on some level, these needs must be met. If these needs are not met, we cannot fulfill our true potential. Ultimately, behaviors are shaped based on meeting these needs, whether it be for the positive or negative.

These are the foundations on which we can build the life we desire. Without the consciousness and understanding of these needs, it is too easy to become overwhelmed by what we think we need rather than by what we really need. By mastering our needs, we can claim balance in our lives. Work through the Reality Checkpoints to find out how to master and understand these needs for yourself.

REALITY CHECKPOINT

1. Write down which two needs you value the most in your life. Let's find out if they are being met in accordance to their value.

    _____ and _____

2. Use the table below to allocate a percentage to each need: one based on how much of the need you would be satisfied to have in your life and OK with, and one based on the reality of where your satisfaction is today.

Table 1

Human Need	What percentage of this need would you need to have in your life to be satisfied?	What percentage of this need do you have in your life as of today?
Variety		
Certainty		
Love & Connection		
Significance		
Growth		
Contribution		

3. Use table 2 to write down all the ways in which you currently meet each need.

Table 2

Human Need	Where in your life are these needs being met?
Variety	
Certainty	
Love & Connection	
Significance	
Growth	
Contribution	

If three or more of your needs are met through the same entity, they are addictions that we may not be aware of. For example, if you wrote that your career is your only way to meet your need for variety, significance, and growth, this indicates that your career has become an addiction. If your career suddenly was missing from your life, you would not be meeting your needs anymore and would need to find a new way to meet the need. This can cause great turmoil. It is important to meet each need through a variety of sources.

4. Write down the impact these needs have on your quality of life.

_____

_____

_____

_____

_____

_____

_____

_____

For Example:
I can see work helps me to meet most of my needs, but I do not make time to spend with family and friends to meet the need of love and connection. Drinking alcohol on the weekends gives me variety; I do it because I'm bored. But it is self-destructive because it affects my relationships, which then stops me from meeting the need of love and connection.

These Reality Checkpoints can add value only if we answer with complete honesty and true reflection. Once these needs have been mastered and we truly understand the depths of what they mean to us, they provide us with a wave of direction and can be an incredible driving force to push toward what we are looking to achieve.

Will Your Real Attitude Please Stand Up?

—oᴇᴏ—

Attitudes are contagious. Is yours worth catching?

—Aɴᴏɴʏᴍᴏᴜꜱ

Hᴀᴠᴇ ʏᴏᴜ ᴇᴠᴇʀ ᴇxᴘᴇʀɪᴇɴᴄᴇᴅ ᴛʜᴇ following scenario? You wake up in the morning in a great mood, feeling like you can take on the world, then begin your commute to work, where it's busy and everyone's rushing around with a miserable look on his or her face, whether it be in traffic or stuck on the train. You finally arrive at work feeling good, but not as great as when you first woke up. Then your boss storms in with a host of jobs for you to do without even a good morning. You take a deep breath and crack on with your day. As you begin drowning in your work, the phone rings; it's a customer complaint, which you deal with in the most professional way, of course. You brush this off and decide it's time for lunch, but you realize you left your food at home. By this point, you're feeling just OK, and you begin to watch the clock until it's time to go home. You arrive home feeling drained and tired after what feels like a crazy long day. The feeling of taking on the world is a distant memory. You have an early night with the intent to wake up to a better tomorrow.

Now, this is a small example of how emotions and attitudes can change based on our environment. The good news is, this can be avoided, and we don't have to be influenced by these things if we take ownership of our attitudes.

Attitudes are one of the main contributors to our character, the way we see our reality, and the way we live our lives. Attitude is a settled way of thinking or feeling about something. It determines the way we feel, influences our behavior, and stems from our beliefs. It is common for others to have an opinion on our attitude—if it needs to be changed or if we are in danger of having an "attitude problem"—because our attitudes differ from theirs. Other people's opinions are only a reflection of themselves.

If we can master our attitudes, they will be there to help us when we slip into autopilot. Thinking and becoming conscious of your current attitude will allow you to see the effects of it. Once you create your desired attitude, you will be playing the game of life on a whole new level.

Next time you find yourself in an undesirable state, *pause*, take a *breath*, and ask yourself the following:

* What am I reacting to?
* Am I jumping to conclusions?
* Is this fact or opinion?
* Am I getting things out of proportion?

- Am I putting more pressure on myself?
- Is there a more effective way of dealing with this?
- What would be the most effective and helpful action to take?

REALITY CHECKPOINT

1. Describe your attitude toward life.
2. How is this attitude serving you positively?
3. Are there any ways in which this attitude is preventing your success?
4. Are there any shifts needed here to help you live more desirably?

Memories

—∽∞∽—

The best memories are the ones
we consciously create.

—KAIZEN LIFE SPARK

WE ALL HAVE MEMORIES—GOOD MEMORIES, bad memories, and every label in between. We already learned that our unconscious mind is
responsible for attaching the meaning to our memories, storing
them, and processing (or not processing) the emotion attached to
them. Many of us remember people telling us stories of the past,
and we trick ourselves into thinking we are actually recalling the moment itself. The mind can store this data in any category it chooses.

Many people say their memories of past experiences hold
them back. They cannot move forward because of this significant
event in their life. Now, this is very true for them because they
really believe it. But what if I told you there was another option?

If we take what we learned about our "reality," we know that a
memory must only be data that we have interpreted. It is we who

have attached the meaning and emotion to the data or to the memory in this scenario. What if we attached a different meaning to the memory? What if we thought about what we learned from these significant memories instead of holding on to a feeling that doesn't serve us?

REALITY CHECKPOINT

1. Use table 3 to write the three most significant memories in your life that shaped who you are today.
2. List the emotions you hold for the memory.
3. Write what you learned from the memory.

Table 3

Memory	Emotions	Learning
Example: Losing a loved one	Example: Sadness, loneliness, grief, anger, fear	Example: It's the cycle of life, we cannot control what happens to us but we can remember what we loved and learned from those we lost. Memories live on the lips of the living. Celebrate life.

Your unconscious mind has processed these memories for you. Reviewing and thinking about what you have learned from the memory and emotion give you the power to consciously process them. You will feel if these memories are holding you back or not. Once we have processed them consciously, we can learn from them. We can take away the power they had over us so it no longer holds us back. If you are still feeling excessively strong emotions every time you think of the memory, this is a sign that you have some unresolved negative emotions that need to be processed. If this is the case, I recommend further work with a coach to assist you in resolving these emotions.

Beliefs

*Whether you think you can or think
you can't, you're right.*

—HENRY FORD

A BELIEF IS ACCEPTING SOMETHING that we deem to be true even if there is no proof. With your newfound understanding of how reality is created and how our conscious versus unconscious mind works, I'm sure you can begin to understand how important it is for our beliefs to be in a place of service to us.

What we believe is how we see the world inside and outside of us. To really make a change in our lives, we must make the decision to change beliefs that do not add value to our lives. These beliefs contribute to our life story, and they drive our behaviors.

Some beliefs are so strong they limit us. Limiting beliefs are false beliefs that are usually made by an incorrect conclusion.

Common limiting beliefs include the following:

* I can't be myself.
* I have too many responsibilities.
* I can't save money.
* I don't have time.
* I can't find love.
* I don't know where to start.
* I can't ask for what I want.
* I can't trust people.
* It's too late to make a change.

All of the above statements may have an element of truth to them in some cases. However, even if some truth exists, action can still be taken. We can look at the facts and be resourceful. We can turn the statements into beliefs that will serve us. The main issue with limiting beliefs is that these statements will be said, and that's where it stops. We don't dig any more to understand how we can change this belief. We simply believe it because the unconscious mind is attracted to the easy option. We must shift our minds to explore new possibilities.

REALITY CHECKPOINT

1. What do you believe about yourself?
2. What would you rather believe about yourself?
3. Write down any beliefs that limit you.

.

Rewriting Your Playbook

———— ∞∞ ————

*Rewriting your playbook will help
you win this game of life.*

—Kaizen Life Spark

Rewriting your playbook incorporates all the MindShift Map strategies and Reality Checkpoints. This section gives you insight into what we call "zones of play" and "states." When we talk about "states," we are referring to our state of mind and body, considering how we feel and how we behave as one. We will encourage you to choose your zones of play and own your states to feel fully empowered. We revisit the Wheel of Spark, setting intentions and visions for the future.

My playbook was nonexistent before Kaizen Life Spark and MindShift Map. I once thought I was calling the shots in my life, but my reality check taught me that it was surface level. I was living the life I had been given, not a life I had designed or created. There was no real depth or longevity to my intentions. I was going with the flow and following a path that others wanted me to be on, not one I had chosen for myself. When I had this realization, I was surprised, defensive, overwhelmed, scared, but excited. Everything I learned had challenged the way I lived my life for all those years. The revelation hit me—I hadn't been wrong all these years; I just wasn't informed. All the strategies and new ways of thinking enhanced the good in the life I once had to bring me the model of the world I choose to see today.

You have already started rewriting your playbook as you have been completing the Reality Checkpoints in this MindShift Map. These strategies open the door to the reality you desire. It's now your choice if you walk through the door. You will start to see your inner world reflecting what you want for your outer world. It's time to ignite the spark and complete your playbook for life. If you are calling the shots, you will win. It is time for your conscious mind to take over, take yourself to another level, and fulfill your true potential.

Going through the playbook, Reality Checkpoints have really helped people to understand that they rely too much on outside influences to create their state of mind. Whether that be happy, calm, or feeling loved, they now know that to create the state they desire comes from within; it comes from a place of choice that is reassuring and empowering.

We do not need permission to write or rewrite the script of our lives. We have the ability to create our own future and our own playbook for life. What will you create?

Being in the Zone

—⊸∞∞⊶—

*The power plant does not have
energy—it generates it.*

—Brendon Burchard

Have you ever felt an emotion or been in a state that you would want to repeat? Have you ever wanted to keep a feeling forever because it felt so good? There is nothing more invigorating than being "in the zone." Being in such a dynamic psychological state can lead to life-changing moments and some of our most precious memories.

If we are the cause of our own results, if we have chosen our reality and woken up to our current position in life, then we absolutely have the capacity to choose our own state.

At any given moment, we can demand our state *if* we have our inner world in order. Our inner world is a sacred place that demands our attention. By choosing and anchoring our desired state, we can reach new levels of mastery in all domains of our lives.

To get "in the zone," we must generate the energy we desire and lead it to the forefront of our being. "In the zone" means different things to different people and will vary depending on what state you are looking for.

For example, you may want to get in a pumped-up, motivated, unstoppable state. Or you may want to get into a loving state after a stressful day at work when you go home to your family. No matter what state you are looking for, you can create it.

REALITY CHECKPOINT

1. Visualize your desired zone.
2. What is the meaning attached to the present moment?
3. Is congruence present in both body and mind? Do you really believe it?
4. Change your physiology and be. Move and strike a powerful posture and embrace the strong emotions you feel.
5. Repeat the steps above to replay your desired state.

For Example:

1. I can see myself calm, still, and smiling contently.
2. I am feeling at peace; this means everything at this moment is exactly how it should be. Nothing else matters.

3. My body feels light, free of any tension, eyes and face relaxed. My mind is clear, with few thoughts running through; there is only space for loving, calm, and grateful thoughts.
4. Stand up tall and inhale deep, raising the arms above the head and stretching the whole body as long as possible. Exhale and bring the arms to center. Do this five times.
5. Every time I want to get into my calm, peaceful zone, I will repeat the above steps.

Owning Your State

---✺✺✺---

One of the early signs of sophistication is not giving
way to all inclinations but rather sending your
emotions to school so they learn how to behave.

—Jim Rohn

State is a combination of emotions and behavior. We can take ownership of our states if we are conscious and willing. Our states drive our behaviors, which in turn impact our reality. What if they could be owned? What if we could be entirely responsible for our states? What if we could be so consistent in our states that we become unshakable? Would you like to learn how to do this? Complete the Reality Checkpoints below, and you'll be aware of how to own *your* state in no time.

Reality Checkpoint

Complete tables 4 and 5 by inserting the following:

1. Write five states you *want* in your life in table 4.
2. Write five states you want to *avoid* in your life in table 5.

3. Write what needs to be in place for you to experience the chosen state.
4. Consider each state and decide if you are in control of it or not.

Table 4

States that you really WANT in your life	What need to be in place for you to experience this?	Am I in control of this being in my life?
Example: Calm	Time with loved ones and time alone	Yes - If I manage my time and ensure I make time

Table 5

States that you really want to AVOID in your life	What need to be in place for you to experience this?	Am I in control of this being in my life?
Example: Stress	Work pressures, relationship pressures	No - I have to work and have relationships. But I can control how I respond to the stress and I can remove myself from stressful situations

The goal is to have as many internal drivers (controlled by you) as possible to create the states you want in life. This allows you to be in control of what is affecting you. If there are many external drivers (controlled by others) in place for you to have your desired states, it is easy to become reliant on things you cannot control. This leads to leaving your state and emotions in the hands of others and playing by others' book of rules and not your own.

For example, if you rely on your job to get the state of excitement and confidence in your life, this is an external driver. If your job was removed from your life, you would no longer have a driver for your confidence and excitement. However, if your confidence came from your own personal development and your excitement came from trips you chose to go on, this would be internal. You would be in full control over your state.

Wheel of Spark of Your Future

Own satisfaction is better than success,
because success is a measure by others, while
satisfaction is a measure decided by us.

—Anonymous

In section 1 of the MindShift Map, you created your own personal Wheel of Spark. You labeled your own wheel with the areas of life that are most important to you. This gave us the reality check of where you are now. We are going to think about the Wheel of Spark with purpose for the future.

Reality Checkpoint

Ensure you have your Wheel of Spark in front of you.

1. Use table 6 to list the areas of your life in order of satisfaction.

63

2. For each area, write why you did not score it a 10 (highest satisfaction).
3. Identify what needs to change for you to become more satisfied in each area.

Use table 7 to assist you.

Table 6

Area of Life (in satisfaction order - Lowest first)	Why did you not score it a 10?	What do I need to change to be more satisfied in this area of my life?

Example:

Table 7

Area of Life (in satisfaction order - Lowest first)	Why did you not score it a 10?	What do I need to change to be more satisfied in this area of my life?
Fun	I rarely have fun anymore. I'm always stuck at work.	Schedule fun outside of work and have fun whilst i'm at work where possible
Rest & Relaxation	I barely get 5 minutes to myself. Other things come first	Make time for myself to relax and unwind. Switch off an hour before bed for me. Book a spa day once a month.
Friends & Family		
Health & Fitness		
Relationship / Romance		
Personal Growth		
Financial		
Career		

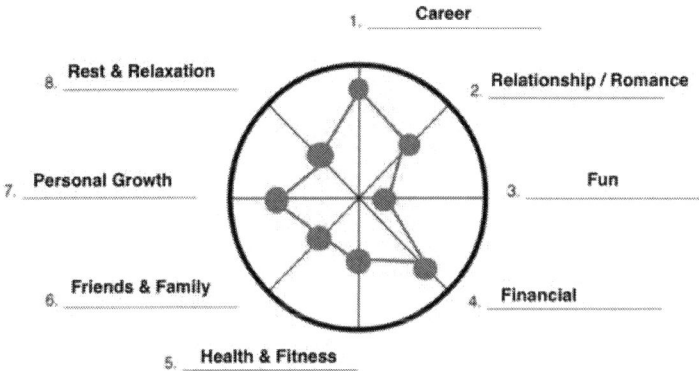

Now that you have completed this exercise, you will have a list of changes you may need to make to become more satisfied in your life. This is the starting point to feel the reality of this satisfaction. It is time to execute.

Vision Setting

—∞∞∞—

*A vision is not just a picture of what could
be; it is an appeal to better ourselves, a
call to become something more.*

—Rosabeth Moss Kanter

Throughout *MindShift Map*, there have been a series of Reality Checkpoints, which I'm sure you have invested the time in completing. The answers you have given to these checkpoints naturally create a vision for your future.

I invite you to complete the final Reality Checkpoint on the MindShift Map journey.

Reality Checkpoint

1. Draw what your desired reality looks like. What colors are there? Who is there? What can you feel? What can you hear? What do you believe? Add as many details as possible.

2. How would you feel if you didn't achieve your desired reality?
3. How will you feel when you achieve your desired reality?
4. How will you know once you've achieved it?
5. Show your drawing and share your vision of your desired reality to another person.
6. Execute your desires.

CONCLUSION

───❈───

THE SPARK OF LIFE AND continuous improvement derives only from within. We started on this journey with a reality check and some eye-opening basics about the potential of the human mind. Together, we have worked through some strategies to understand your own life story and to create your playbook for life.

This is your first step into the world of Kaizen Life Spark and *your* model of the world. Many will read *MindShift Map* without completing the Reality Checkpoints, and that's OK—that's where they are in their journey. Even by reading the information, we cannot help but be affected, which is simply magical.

However, most of you have completed the checkpoints and have given yourself the personal power to have your own playbook for the future. Congratulations to you! Simply knowing we have the choice to affect our reality is all we need. To take action from our knowing will accelerate your levels of love, growth, success, and contribution in this world.

For further support and inspiration or for another Kaizen Life Spark experience, please visit www.kaizenlifespark.com. You will be able to find resources I have created for you on your journey. The journey ahead will be a fruitful one. Some days, you will rise with a flame of purpose; other days, you will need to reignite that spark. Either way, you are well equipped for anything life throws at you. After all, it is all a reflection of your model of the world.

Unconditional love and gratitude,

Kaizen Life Spark

ABOUT THE AUTHOR

CHARLOTTE MILLS IS THE FOUNDER of Kaizen Life Spark and author of *MindShift Map*. She is also the creator of the online coaching platform that has helped many people ignite the spark in their lives and started them on their journey to a more fulfilled life.

Charlotte has been in the world of coaching since 2005 in wellness and fitness, helping people to reach their physical and lifestyle goals. Charlotte became extremely passionate about the psychological aspects of coaching as well as the physical elements.

In 2014, Kaizen Life Spark was born and has evolved into what it is today. Charlotte dedicates her life to helping others and shares her struggles, successes, and strategies to enhance their results. Charlotte has taken what she has learned from personal experiences, client experiences, and mentors and created a coaching method that can take ordinary lives to extraordinary.

Meet Charlotte and receive free training and resources at kaizenlifespark.com.

PLAYBOOK JOURNAL PAGES

⸺⧓⸺

....
....
....
....
....
....
....
....
....
....
....
....
....
....
....
....
....
....
....
....
....
....

....
....
....
....
....
....
....
....
....
....
....
....
....
....
....
....
....
....
....
....
....
....
....
....
....
....
....
....

PLAYBOOK JOURNAL PAGES

....
....
....
....
....
....
....
....
....
....
....
....
....
....
....
....
....
....
....
....

PLAYBOOK JOURNAL PAGES

———⚬⚬⚬———

....
....
....
....
....
....
....
....
....
....
....
....
....
....
....
....
....
....
....
....

PLAYBOOK JOURNAL PAGES

—∞∞∞—

....
....
....
....
....
....
....
....
....
....
....
....
....
....
....
....
....
....
....
....
....

PLAYBOOK JOURNAL PAGES

···
···
···
···
···
···
···
···
···
···
···
···
···
···
···
···
···
···
···
···
···

....
....
....
....
....
....
....
....
....
....
....
....
....
....
....
....
....
....
....
....
....
....
....
....
....
....
....
....
....
....

Printed in Great Britain
by Amazon